Moving into English

School-Home Resources

Grade 2

Harcourt

Orlando   Austin   Chicago   New York   Toronto   London   San Diego

Visit *The Learning Site!*
www.harcourtschool.com

CONTENTS

Take-Home Books

Unit 1	Lesson 1	Fly, Little Duck!
	Lesson 2	The Birthday Picnic
	Lesson 3	New School, New Friends
	Lesson 4	The Peach Farm
Unit 2	Lesson 6	Where Is Max?
	Lesson 7	Our New House
	Lesson 8	The Pet Store
	Lesson 9	Bunny's Big Mistake
Unit 3	Lesson 11	The Field Trip
	Lesson 12	Weather Report
	Lesson 13	Camping Trip
	Lesson 14	Marcy's Lemon Tree
Unit 4	Lesson 16	I Love to Draw
	Lesson 17	Andy Plays the Guitar
	Lesson 18	A Trip to the Desert
	Lesson 19	Joe's Problem
Unit 5	Lesson 21	Our Holiday Trip
	Lesson 22	Lou's Bus
	Lesson 23	A Walk in the Forest
	Lesson 24	Rosie Flamingo
Unit 6	Lesson 26	Faraway Places
	Lesson 27	Brother Moon, Sister Star
	Lesson 28	Dear Anna
	Lesson 29	Grandma's Chair

Dear Family Member,

Welcome to *Moving into English*! Each week you will receive a letter that suggests activities to go with what your child is reading in English. Encourage your child to write the title "My Family Book" on a small notebook and decorate the cover. Then each week you and your child can write something to remember, from what you talk about. You can do this in your home language or in English.

This week your child read a story about feelings. Talk with your child in your home language about feelings he or she has. This will help your child understand that it's all right for people to have different feelings at different times.

In the Family Book, write *I feel happy when* _____. You and your child can each complete the sentence in your own way.

We hope you and your child will enjoy talking and writing about feelings.

Dear Family Member,

This week your child learned English words for family members by reading a poem about a family picnic. Talk with your child about family members he or she has met. Tell your child about family parties you went to when you were a child. Speaking in your home language about the members of your family can help your child remember who is who.

In the Family Book, write about one of your family members and invite your child to do the same. A photo from a family picnic or party would be fun to add!

We hope you and your child will enjoy talking about your family.

Estimado miembro de la familia:

Bienvenido a *Moving into English*! Cada semana recibirá una carta en la que le sugeriremos actividades relacionadas con lo que su hijo está leyendo en inglés. Motive a su hijo a que escriba el título *"My Family Book"* ("Mi libro de la familia") en una libreta pequeña y que decore la cubierta. Cada semana su hijo y usted pueden escribir algo en su idioma natal o en inglés que les recuerde lo que hablaron.

Esta semana su hijo está leyendo un cuento acerca de los sentimientos. Hablen en su idioma natal acerca de los sentimientos de su hijo. Esto le ayudará a comprender que es normal que los sentimientos varíen según la ocasión.

En el Libro de la familia, escriba: *I feel happy when* _____. (Me siento feliz cuando _____.) Su hijo y usted pueden completar la oración por separado.

Esperamos que disfruten de hablar y escribir acerca de los sentimientos.

Estimado miembro de la familia:

Esta semana su hijo está aprendiendo palabras en inglés para referirse a miembros de la familia mientras lee un poema acerca de un pícnic. Hable con su hijo acerca de los miembros de la familia que él o ella haya conocido. Cuéntele acerca de fiestas familiares a las que usted iba cuando era niño. Hablar en su idioma natal acerca de los miembros de su familia puede ayudar a su hijo a recordar quién es cada uno.

En el Libro de la familia, escriba acerca de uno de sus familiares e invite a su hijo a que haga lo mismo. Resultaría divertido incluir una foto de un pícnic o una fiesta familiar.

Esperamos que disfruten de hablar acerca de su familia.

Dear Family Member,

This week your child read about a boy who tells his uncle about things he does with his friends. At the end the boy decides that his dog is his very best friend.

Talk with your child about the things he or she does with friends. If you have a dog, you and your child could take the dog out for a walk while you chat.

In the Family Book, write about a friend or a pet you had when you were a child. Then ask your child to write a sentence or two about one of his or her friends.

We hope you enjoy these conversations and experiences with your child.

Dear Family Member,

This week your child read about the things people need to live. These include food, water, shelter, air, and the love of friends and family.

Talk with your child about things we want, such as a new toy, and things we really need, such as water. Talking in your home language about the difference between *wanting* and *needing* can help your child recognize what he or she already has.

In the Family Book, write this sentence: *We need _____ to live.* Have your child write a real need in the blank. He or she can then draw a picture to go with the sentence.

Estimado miembro de la familia:

Esta semana su hijo está aprendiendo inglés mientras lee acerca de un niño que le cuenta a su tío lo que hace con sus amigos. Al final, el niño decide que, de todos, su perro es su mejor amigo.

Hable con su hijo acerca de las cosas que él o ella hace con sus amigos. Si tienen un perro, su hijo y usted pueden sacarlo a pasear mientras conversan.

En el Libro de la familia, escriba acerca de un amigo o mascota que usted haya tenido durante su niñez. Luego pida a su hijo que escriba una o dos oraciones acerca de sus amigos.

Esperamos que disfruten de estas conversaciones y experiencias.

Estimado miembro de la familia:

Esta semana su hijo está aprendiendo inglés mientras lee acerca de las cosas que las personas necesitan para vivir, como comida, agua, albergue, aire y el amor de amigos y familiares.

Hable con su hijo acerca de las cosas que queremos, como un juguete nuevo, y las cosas que en realidad necesitamos, como el agua. Hablar en su idioma natal acerca de la diferencia entre *querer* y *necesitar* puede ayudar a su hijo a reconocer lo que ya tiene.

En el Libro de la familia, escriba la siguiente oración: *We need _____ to live.* (Necesitamos _____ para vivir). Pida a su hijo que escriba una necesidad real en el espacio en blanco. También puede hacer un dibujo que vaya con la oración.

Dear Family Member,

This week your child read a play based on an old tale, "The Lion and the Mouse." The lion is surprised to learn that even a little friend can be a big help.

Encourage your child to tell you the story about the lion and the mouse. Perhaps there is a similar tale in your home language that you can tell your child.

In the Family Book, write about a time when someone helped you solve a problem. Then invite your child to add to your story or to draw a picture for it.

We hope you will enjoy sharing stories with your child.

Dear Family Member,

This week your child read about a boy who helps on his family's ranch. Compare the things the boy does on the ranch with the things your child is asked to do in your home. Talking in your home language can help your child understand how important it is for each family member to do his or her part.

If you live on a ranch or have visited one, write in the Family Book something you like about ranches, and ask your child to do the same. If your child has never been to a ranch, invite him or her to write about the boy in the story.

We hope you enjoy talking with your child about life on a ranch.

Estimado miembro de la familia:

Esta semana su hijo está aprendiendo inglés mientras lee una obra de teatro basada en el viejo cuento *"The Lion and the Mouse"* ("El león y el ratón"). El león se sorprende al aprender que incluso un pequeño amigo puede ser de gran ayuda.

Motive a su hijo a contarle el cuento del león y el ratón. Quizás sepa otro cuento similar en su idioma natal que le pueda contar a su hijo.

En el Libro de la familia, escriba acerca de una ocasión en la que alguien lo haya sorprendido al ayudarlo a resolver un problema. Luego invite a su hijo a que contribuya al relato o haga un dibujo al respecto.

Esperamos que disfrute de compartir cuentos con su hijo.

Estimado miembro de la familia:

Esta semana su hijo está aprendiendo inglés mientras lee acerca de un niño que ayuda en el rancho de su familia. Compare las tareas del niño en el rancho con las tareas que tiene su hijo en su hogar. Hablar en su idioma natal puede ayudar a su hijo a entender cuán importante es que cada miembro de la familia cumpla con sus obligaciones.

Si usted vive en un rancho o ha visitado alguno, escriba en el Libro de la familia algo que le guste acerca de los ranchos y pida a su hijo que haga lo mismo. Si su hijo nunca ha estado en un rancho, pídale que escriba acerca del niño del cuento.

Esperamos que disfruten de conversar acerca de la vida en un rancho.

Dear Family Member,

This week your child read about how buildings are made. The selection shows machines that the workers use, such as concrete mixers, cranes, and bulldozers.

Talk in your home language about the many people who must work together to make a building. If possible, take your child to see a construction site.

With your child, write about something you saw at the building site or have seen in the past. If your child is interested in the machinery, encourage him or her to draw and write about a bulldozer, a crane, or another machine.

We hope your child will enjoy telling other family members what he or she learned about construction.

Dear Family Member,

This week your child read about the work of a veterinarian. In the selection Dr. Smith explains how she examines cats, dogs, and other pets at an animal shelter.

Talk with your child about veterinarians and how they take care of pets. If you have a family pet, you might talk about times when you have taken it to a veterinarian.

In the Family Book, look back at what you and your child wrote in Lesson 4 about the things people need to live. Help your child understand that pets have the same needs. Help your child write a pair of sentences such as *We need to drink water to live. Cats need water to live, too.*

Ask your child whether he or she might like to become a veterinarian someday, and why or why not.

Estimado miembro de la familia:

Esta semana su hijo está aprendiendo inglés mientras lee un artículo acerca de cómo se construyen edificios. El artículo enseña las máquinas que usan los obreros, como las mezcladoras de hormigón, grúas y bulldozers.

Hable en su idioma natal acerca de la cantidad de personas que deben trabajar en conjunto para construir un edificio. Si es posible, lleve a su hijo a ver una obra de construcción.

Con su hijo, escriba acerca de algo que vio en la obra de construcción o que haya visto anteriormente. Si a su hijo le interesan las máquinas, motívelo a que escriba o dibuje acerca de un bulldozer, una grúa u otro aparato.

Esperamos que su hijo disfrute de contarles a otros familiares lo que aprendió acerca de construcción.

Estimado miembro de la familia:

Esta semana su hijo está aprendiendo inglés mientras lee acerca de las labores de un veterinario. En el artículo, la Dra. Smith explica cómo examina gatos, perros y otras mascotas en un albergue para animales.

Hable con su hijo acerca de los veterinarios y de cómo cuidan a los animales. Si tienen una mascota, pueden hablar acerca de las veces en que la han llevado al veterinario.

En el Libro de la familia, busquen lo que escribieron en la Lección 4 sobre lo que se necesita para vivir. Ayude a su hijo a comprender que las mascotas tienen las mismas necesidades. Ayúdelo a escribir un par de oraciones como: *We need to drink water to live. Cats need water to live, too.* (Necesitamos beber agua para vivir. Los gatos también necesitan agua para vivir.)

Pregunte a su hijo si le gustaría ser veterinario algún día y por qué.

Dear Family Member,

This week's story comes from the old rhyme, "Humpty Dumpty." Little Lumpty, an egg, climbs to the top of the town wall. When he can't get back down, his family and friends work together to save him.

Ask your child to tell how Little Lumpty was saved from falling off the wall.

Talk about real-life helpers, such as firefighters, who work together.

Then add to the Family Book. Write about a group of helpers that you admire. Ask your child to add something to what you wrote and draw a picture.

We hope you and your child will enjoy these activities.

Dear Family Member,

This week your child learned English from an old folktale. The Little Red Hen works hard baking bread with no help from her friends. When they smell her fresh bread and want to eat it, she says no. They then realize they should have helped their friend, so they offer to help with the cleanup.

Talk with your child about ways your whole family can work together. Perhaps you can all bake something good to eat. Working together and chatting in your home language about cooking will be fun for all of you.

In the Family Book, help your child write a sentence or two about cooking together or another project the family has done.

We hope you and your child have fun working together.

Estimado miembro de la familia:

El cuento de esta semana está basado en la vieja rima *"Humpty Dumpty"*. Little Lumpty, un huevo, se trepa a la pared del pueblo. Al no poderse bajar, sus amigos trabajan en conjunto para rescatarlo.

Pida a su hijo que le cuente cómo salvaron a Little Lumpty para que no se cayera de la pared.

Hablen acerca de ayudantes de la vida real que trabajan en conjunto, como los bomberos.

En el Libro de la familia, escriba acerca de un grupo de ayudantes que usted admire. Pida a su hijo que contribuya al relato y haga un dibujo.

Esperamos que disfruten de estas actividades.

Estimado miembro de la familia:

Esta semana su hijo está aprendiendo inglés mientras lee un viejo cuento tradicional. La Gallinita Roja se esmera en hornear pan sin contar con la ayuda de sus amigos. Cuando huelen el pan recién horneado y quieren probarlo, ella les dice que no. Ellos se dan cuenta de que debieron de haber ayudado a su amiga y se ofrecen a ayudar con la limpieza.

Hable con su hijo acerca de maneras en que la familia entera puede trabajar junta. Quizás puedan hornear algo delicioso para comer. Trabajar juntos y hablar acerca de cocinar en su idioma natal será divertido para todos.

En el Libro de la familia, ayude a su hijo a escribir una o dos oraciones acerca de cocinar juntos o de otro proyecto en el que haya participado la familia.

Esperamos que disfruten de trabajar juntos.

Dear Family Member,

This week your child read about the city of El Paso, Texas. El Paso began as a mission. It started to grow when the railroad arrived. Later a dam was built, and El Paso grew into a large, modern city.

If you live in or near El Paso, you and your child will have a lot to talk about. If not, help your child find the city on a map, and talk about ways El Paso is like and different from the place where you live. Ask older friends how your area has changed over the years.

In the Family Book, write one or two interesting facts you and your child have found out about El Paso or about your own community.

We hope you and your child will enjoy learning more about where you live.

Dear Family Member,

This week your child read about four types of storms: thunderstorms, hurricanes, tornados, and blizzards. The selection also tells how to prepare for each storm and how to stay safe when it comes.

You and other family members probably have stories about storms you remember. Sharing these stories in your home language will help your child understand that there are ways to cope with dangerous weather.

Choose a type of storm that you might get in your area. Talk with your child about ways to be safe in such a storm. Then work together to write a list of safety rules in the Family Book.

Estimado miembro de la familia:

Esta semana su hijo está leyendo acerca de la ciudad de El Paso, Texas. El Paso primero fue una misión. Comenzó a crecer con la llegada del ferrocarril. Luego se construyó una represa y El Paso se convirtió en una ciudad grande y moderna.

Si vive en o cerca de El Paso, su hijo y usted tendrán mucho de qué hablar. De lo contrario, ayude a su hijo a encontrar la ciudad en un mapa y hablen acerca de las maneras en que El Paso se asemeja o diferencia del lugar donde viven. Pregunte a amistades de edad avanzada cómo el área donde ustedes viven ha cambiado con el pasar de los años.

En el Libro de la familia, escriba uno o dos datos interesantes que su hijo y usted hayan averiguado acerca de El Paso o su comunidad.

Esperamos que disfruten de aprender más acerca del lugar donde viven.

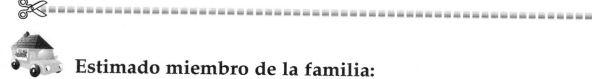

Estimado miembro de la familia:

Esta semana su hijo está aprendiendo inglés mientras lee acerca de cuatro tipos de tormenta: tormenta eléctrica, huracán, tornado y ventisca. El artículo también indica cómo prepararse para cada tormenta y mantenerse a salvo durante la misma.

Puede que usted y otros familiares tengan algo que contar acerca de tormentas pasadas. Compartir estas historias en su idioma natal ayudará a su hijo a comprender que hay maneras de lidiar con estados de tiempo peligrosos.

Seleccione un tipo de tormenta que ocurra en su área. Hable con su hijo acerca de las medidas de seguridad que se deben tomar durante este tipo de tormenta. Luego escriban una lista de reglas de seguridad en el Libro de la familia.

© Harcourt

Dear Family Member,

This week your child read more about weather. He or she learned English by reading poems about rain and snow.

Talk with your child about why the puddles you see after it rains disappear when the sun comes out. Explain that the puddle evaporates into the air as the water turns back into a gas. Have your child put some water into a clear container. Mark the water level. Leave the cup on a windowsill, and check the water level the next day to see how much water has evaporated.

In the Family Book, help your child write about what you did and what happened.

Dear Family Member,

This week your child read a story about a girl who wants to grow a flower. She tries many things, but the flower won't grow until it gets the sun and rain it needs.

Talk with your child about flowers you have grown or flowers you see growing in your neighborhood. Perhaps you and your child can take a "flower walk" and name the flowers you see.

In the Family Book, work together to draw your favorite flowers and write a sentence about each.

We hope you will enjoy these flower activities with your child.

Estimado miembro de la familia:

Esta semana su hijo está leyendo más acerca del estado del tiempo. Está aprendiendo inglés mientras lee poemas acerca de la lluvia y la nieve.

Hable con su hijo de por qué los charcos que se forman después que llueve desaparecen al salir el sol. Explique que los charcos se evaporan en el aire a medida que el agua retorna a su estado gaseoso. Pida a su hijo que agregue agua a un envase transparente. Marque el nivel del agua. Coloque el envase en la repisa de la ventana y verifique el nivel del agua al día siguiente para ver la cantidad de agua que se ha evaporado.

En el Libro de la familia, ayude a su hijo a escribir acerca de lo que hicieron y de lo que ocurrió.

- -

Estimado miembro de la familia:

Esta semana su hijo está aprendiendo inglés mientras lee un cuento acerca de una niña que quiere cultivar una flor. Ella intenta muchas cosas, pero la flor no crece hasta que recibe el sol y la lluvia que necesita.

Hable con su hijo acerca de flores que han cultivado o que estén creciendo en su vecindario. Quizás quieran dar un "paseo entre flores" y nombrar las flores que vean.

En el Libro de la familia dibujen sus flores favoritas y escriban una oración acerca de cada una.

Esperamos que disfruten de estas actividades con flores.

Dear Family Member,

This week your child read a play about an apple seed that wants to grow. Snow is covering the ground, so the seed can't grow yet. The seed asks the rain and the wind for help, but only the sun is able to make the snow go away.

If you do not get snow in your area, you may need to explain to your child that snow will melt when the temperature gets above freezing. You and your child might want to put ice out in the sun to show how snow melts into water.

In the Family Book, work with your child to write a sentence or two about something you like to do in the snow. If you do not have snow where you live, write about something you would like to try if you could visit a snowy area.

We hope you and your child will enjoy your conversations about snow and other kinds of weather.

Dear Family Member,

This week your child read about how author Loreen Leedy creates a picture book. The selection tells how the author does research, sketches the characters, plans the book, and writes the story. Like many authors today, Loreen Leedy uses a computer for much of her work.

Perhaps you and your child can borrow some picture books from the library and look at them carefully. Talking in your home language about a well-done book will help your child understand that being creative takes work but is worth the effort.

In the Family Book, invite your child to draw a character that could be the star of a picture book and to write a book title. If you have a computer, your child might want to try using a drawing program.

We hope you will enjoy this exercise in creativity with your child.

Estimado miembro de la familia:

Esta semana su hijo está aprendiendo inglés mientras lee una obra de teatro acerca de una semilla de manzana que quiere crecer. La nieve está cubriendo el suelo, por lo que la semilla no puede crecer todavía. La semilla le pide a la lluvia y al viento que la ayuden, pero sólo el Sol es capaz de lograr que la nieve se vaya.

Si no nieva en su área, quizás necesite explicarle a su hijo que la nieve se derretirá cuando la temperatura suba. Pueden colocar hielo al sol para demostrar cómo la nieve se derrite y se convierte en agua.

En el Libro de la familia, escriban una o dos oraciones acerca de algo que les guste hacer en la nieve. Si no nieva en su área, escriban acerca de algo que les gustaría hacer si visitaran un lugar con nieve.

Esperamos que hayan disfrutado de sus conversaciones acerca de la nieve y otros elementos climatológicos.

- -

Estimado miembro de la familia:

Esta semana su hijo está leyendo acerca de cómo la autora Loreen Leedy crea un libro ilustrado. En el artículo se indica cómo la autora investiga, hace bocetos de los personajes, planifica el libro y escribe el cuento. Como muchos autores de hoy, Loreen Leedy lleva a cabo gran parte de su trabajo en la computadora.

Quizás puedan tomar prestados libros ilustrados de la biblioteca para observarlos con cuidado. Hablar en su idioma natal acerca de un libro bien hecho ayudará a su hijo a entender que la creatividad cuesta trabajo, pero vale la pena.

En el Libro de la familia, invite a su hijo a dibujar un personaje que podría ser la estrella de un libro ilustrado y a que escriba un título para el libro. Si tiene computadora, motive a su hijo a que utilice un programa de dibujo.

Esperamos que disfruten de este ejercicio creativo.

Dear Family Member,

This week your child read a story about two good friends, Frog and Toad. Toad tries to think of a story to tell Frog, but he can't come up with anything. Then Frog tells his own story about Toad's efforts to think of a story.

Talk with your child about ways to get story ideas. You might choose something special where you live—a statue, a painting on a building, an unusual cactus or other plant—and think of a story you could tell about it. Chatting about story ideas in your home language can help your child get story ideas in his or her English class, too.

You and your child can work together to create the story you thought of. Write the story in the Family Book for others to enjoy.

We hope you and your child will find many ways to use your imagination.

Dear Family Member,

This week your child read about how Maria Montoya Martinez, a famous potter in New Mexico, kept Pueblo pottery traditions alive.

Think of artists from your own culture. Talk with your child about one or more artists you admire. If possible, borrow books from the library that show examples of the work of those artists. Conversations in your home language about their art will help your child know more about your culture.

Write about one of those artists in the Family Book. Encourage your child to add to what you write by telling what he or she likes about a particular work of art.

We hope you will enjoy talking with your child about creative people who keep alive traditions from your cultural heritage.

Estimado miembro de la familia:

Esta semana su hijo está aprendiendo inglés mientras lee un cuento acerca de dos buenos amigos, Frog y Toad (Rana y Sapo). Sapo intenta inventar un cuento para contárselo a Rana, pero no se le ocurre nada. Luego Rana se inventa un cuento acerca de los esfuerzos de Sapo.

Hable con su hijo acerca de maneras de obtener ideas para escribir cuentos. Pueden seleccionar algo especial donde viven (una estatua, un mural, un cacto u otra planta inusual) y pensar en una historia que se pueda contar al respecto. Hablar acerca de ideas para cuentos en su idioma natal puede ayudar a que su hijo también obtenga ideas para cuentos en la clase de inglés.

Pueden crear el cuento en el que pensaron. Escríbanlo en el Libro de la familia para el disfrute de todos.

Esperamos que encuentren muchas maneras para utilizar su imaginación.

Estimado miembro de la familia:

Esta semana su hijo está leyendo acerca de como María Montoya Martínez, una alfarera famosa de Nuevo México, mantuvo vivas las tradiciones de alfarería de la cultura pueblo.

Piense en un artista de su cultura. Hable con su hijo acerca de uno o más artistas que admire. Si es posible, tome prestados libros de la biblioteca que muestren ejemplos de las obras de esos artistas. Conversaciones en su idioma natal acerca de dicho arte ayudará a su hijo a conocer mejor su cultura.

Escriba acerca de uno de los artistas en el Libro de la familia. Motive a su hijo a que contribuya al escrito expresando lo que le gusta sobre una obra de arte en particular.

Esperamos que disfruten de compartir opiniones acerca de personas creativas que mantienen vivas sus tradiciones culturales.

Dear Family Member,

This week your child read a story about the many wonderful things hands can do. The boy in the story decides that when he grows up, he will use his hands to help and to create.

Talk with your child in your home language about things you and other family members like to do with your hands. Discuss how important your hands are for doing almost everything in life.

In the Family Book, write about something you do with your hands. Have your child do the same. Then work together to write about how other family members use their hands.

We hope that you will enjoy thinking about ways that hands help us create things and do many important jobs.

Dear Family Member,

This week your child read a play. A king tells his people that the person who gives him the best gift will rule his kingdom after him. Many people buy him expensive gifts, but the winner is a girl who gives him a picture she has drawn herself.

Ask your child why he or she thinks the king chose the gift that the girl made herself, instead of an expensive store-bought gift. Discussing gift-giving in your home language will help your child understand that the best gifts are those made with love.

In the Family Book, start a list of gifts that you could make for others. Ask your child to write more suggestions for the list. You might enjoy choosing one of the ideas and making a gift for someone you know.

We hope you and your child will enjoy talking about gift-giving.

Estimado miembro de la familia:

Esta semana su hijo está aprendiendo inglés mientras lee un cuento acerca de las maravillas que se pueden hacer con las manos. El niño del cuento decide que cuando sea mayor, usará sus manos para ayudar y crear.

Hable con su hijo en su idioma natal acerca de las cosas que a usted y otros familiares les gusta hacer con las manos. Hablen acerca de cuán importante son las manos para hacer casi todo en la vida.

En el Libro de la familia, escriba acerca de algo que haga con las manos. Pida a su hijo que escriba sobre lo mismo. Luego trabajen juntos para escribir sobre cómo otros familiares usan las manos.

Esperamos que disfruten de pensar en maneras en que las manos nos ayudan a crear y llevar a cabo trabajos importantes.

Estimado miembro de la familia:

Esta semana su hijo está aprendiendo inglés mientras lee una obra de teatro. El Rey le dice a su pueblo que la persona que le traiga el mejor obsequio reinará después de él. Muchos le compran obsequios costosos, pero gana una niña que le regala un dibujo hecho por ella misma.

Pregunte a su hijo por qué piensa que el Rey seleccionó el obsequio que la niña había hecho, en vez de un obsequio costoso comprado en una tienda. Hablar en su idioma natal acerca del acto de obsequiar ayudará a su hijo a comprender que los mejores regalos son aquellos hechos con amor.

En el Libro de la familia, comience una lista de regalos hechos en casa. Pida a su hijo que añada más sugerencias a la lista. Quizás les resulte divertido seleccionar una de las ideas y hacerla en casa para regalársela a otra persona.

Esperamos que disfruten del acto de obsequiar.

Dear Family Member,

This week your child learned about three American holidays: Flag Day, Independence Day, and Presidents' Day.

Every nation has patriotic holidays that celebrate events in its history. Ask your child to tell you about the American holidays he or she has just read about. Tell your child in your home language about holidays that are celebrated in your home country.

Help your child compare an American holiday with a similar holiday in your home country—for example, Independence Day. With your child, write facts about each of the holidays in your Family Book. This will help your child feel proud to be connected to both countries.

Dear Family Member,

This week your child read about and talked about neighborhood helpers such as police officers, mail carriers, librarians, doctors and nurses, and teachers.

Take your child for a walk around your neighborhood and talk about the community helpers you see. Conversations in your home language enrich your child's understanding of the world around him or her.

In the Family Book, write about a community helper you knew about when you were a child. Then help your child write about a community helper in your neighborhood.

We hope you enjoy these conversations and experiences with your child.

Estimado miembro de la familia:

Esta semana su hijo está aprendiendo acerca de tres días festivos de Estados Unidos: el Día de los Presidentes, el Día de la Bandera y el Día de la Independencia.

Cada nación celebra fiestas patrias para conmemorar sucesos históricos. Pida a su hijo que le cuente acerca de los días festivos estadounidenses que acaba de leer. En su idioma natal, cuéntele acerca de los días festivos que celebran en su país de origen.

Ayude a su hijo a comparar un día festivo estadounidense con uno similar de su país de origen (por ejemplo, el Día de la Independencia). Escriban datos acerca de cada uno de estos días festivos en el Libro de la familia para ayudar a su hijo a sentirse orgulloso de estar conectado con ambos países.

Estimado miembro de la familia:

Esta semana su hijo está aprendiendo inglés mientras lee y habla acerca de ayudantes comunitarios como policías, carteros, bibliotecarios, doctores, enfermeros y maestros.

Salga a caminar con su hijo por su vecindario y hable con los ayudantes comunitarios que vea. Conversar en su idioma natal enriquece la comprensión de su hijo hacia el mundo que lo rodea.

En el Libro de la familia, escriba acerca de un ayudante comunitario que conoció durante su niñez y ayude a su hijo a escribir acerca de un ayudante de su vecindario.

Esperamos que disfruten de estas conversaciones y experiencias.

Dear Family Member,

This week your child read an article about the different kinds of animals that may live in an oak tree over time.

You and your child have talked about the way people in communities depend on one another. Living things in nature also depend on one another. Ask your child to explain how the oak tree could be called a community.

Choose a nearby tree or a large cactus, and watch the animals that come and go for a day or two. In the Family Book, help your child write about this community of nature.

We hope you and your child will enjoy thinking about communities in this way.

Dear Family Member,

This week your child read about a community of emperor penguins. Ask your child to share with the family some interesting facts about penguins. For example: penguin fathers share the work of taking care of their baby penguins. You may want to check out some library books about penguins, too.

In the Family Book, write something new that you learned about penguins. Have your child add more facts about penguins and draw a picture.

We hope the whole family will find penguins interesting.

Estimado miembro de la familia:

Esta semana su hijo está aprendiendo inglés mientras lee un artículo acerca de los diferentes tipos de animales que llegan a habitar un roble.

Han conversado sobre la manera en que los miembros de una comunidad dependen unos de otros. Los seres que habitan en la naturaleza también dependen unos de otros. Pida a su hijo que explique por qué se podría decir que el roble es una comunidad.

Seleccione un árbol o cacto grande cerca de ustedes y durante uno o dos días observen los animales que lo visitan. En el Libro de la familia, ayude a su hijo a escribir acerca de esta comunidad de la naturaleza.

Esperamos que disfruten de pensar en las comunidades de esta manera.

Estimado miembro de la familia:

Esta semana su hijo está aprendiendo inglés mientras lee acerca de una comunidad de pingüinos emperadores. Pida a su hijo que comparta con la familia datos interesantes acerca de los pingüinos. Por ejemplo: el pingüino macho comparte la labor de cuidar a sus hijos. También pueden buscar libros acerca de los pingüinos en la biblioteca.

En el Libro de la familia, escriba un dato nuevo que haya aprendido acerca de los pingüinos. Pida a su hijo que añada más datos y que haga un dibujo.

Esperamos que la familia entera encuentre a los pingüinos interesantes.

© Harcourt

25

Dear Family Member,

This week your child read a play about a girl who is looking for her dog, Buttons. At the end, the girl finds Buttons in time for them to join in the town parade.

Talk with your child about parades he or she has seen and about parades you remember from your childhood. Such a conversation in your home language will help your child understand that parades are a way people show pride in their community.

In the Family Book, have your child write what he or she would like to do in a parade and draw a picture to show it.

We hope you and your child will enjoy talking about parades.

26

Dear Family Member,

This week your child read about places a family visits on vacation: the Alamo, the state capitol in Austin, the Johnson Space Center, the Port Isabel lighthouse, Palo Duro Canyon, El Paso, and Big Bend National Park.

Talk with your child about these places, and help him or her find each place on a map of Texas. Chatting in your home language about places to visit will increase your child's interest in your state.

Choose a place you have visited or would like to visit. Write a sentence or two in the Family Book about that place. Then ask your child to do the same for another place.

We hope your family will enjoy using a map and talking about travels.

© Harcourt

Estimado miembro de la familia:

Esta semana su hijo está leyendo una obra de teatro acerca de una niña que está buscando a su perro. Al final, la niña encuentra a Buttons justo a tiempo para unirse al desfile del pueblo.

Hable con su hijo acerca de los desfiles que él o ella haya visto y los que usted recuerde de su niñez. Llevar a cabo esta conversación en su idioma natal ayudará a su hijo a comprender que los desfiles son una manera de demostrar orgullo por una comunidad.

Pida a su hijo que escriba lo que le gustaría hacer en un desfile y que haga un dibujo al respecto en el Libro de la familia.

Esperamos que disfruten de hablar acerca de desfiles.

25

26

Estimado miembro de la familia:

Esta semana su hijo está aprendiendo inglés mientras lee acerca de los lugares que una familia visita en sus vacaciones: el Álamo, el capitolio en Austin, el Centro Espacial Johnson, el faro Port Isabel, el cañón Palo Duro, El Paso y el Parque Nacional Big Bend.

Hable con su hijo acerca de estos lugares y ayúdelo a encontrar cada lugar en un mapa de Texas. Hablar en su idioma natal acerca de lugares para visitar aumentará el interés de su hijo en su estado.

Seleccione un lugar que haya visitado o le gustaría visitar. Escriba una o dos oraciones acerca del lugar. Luego pida a su hijo que haga lo mismo para otro lugar.

Esperamos que su familia disfrute de usar un mapa y hablar de viajes.

© Harcourt

Dear Family Member,

This week your child learned English from a folktale about a silver baboon. The baboon rescues a star and is rewarded by the sun and the moon.

After dark on a clear night, take your child outside to look at the stars. See if you can find some star pictures and the North Star. Talking about the night sky in your home language will help your child know what he or she is seeing.

In the Family Book, you and your child can each write about looking at the stars.

We hope your family will enjoy exploring the night sky.

Dear Family Member,

This week your child read about two American brothers, Wilbur and Orville Wright, who invented an airplane that could really fly.

In your home language, talk with your child about what it takes to invent something new—creativity, imagination, and sometimes bravery, as in the case of the Wright brothers.

In the Family Book, have your child draw and write about what he or she would like to invent. Encourage your child to use imagination—the invention doesn't have to be realistic.

We hope you and your child will enjoy thinking of possible new inventions.

Estimado miembro de la familia:

Esta semana su hijo está aprendiendo inglés de un cuento tradicional acerca del cielo nocturno. Un babuino se ingenia la manera de rescatar a una estrella, por lo que el Sol y la Luna lo recompensan.

En una noche clara, salga con su hijo a ver las estrellas. Vea si pueden reconocer constelaciones y la Estrella del Norte. Hablar acerca del cielo nocturno en su idioma natal ayudará a su hijo a saber sobre lo que está viendo.

En el Libro de la familia, escriban por separado acerca de observar estrellas.

Esperamos que su familia disfrute de explorar el cielo nocturno.

Estimado miembro de la familia:

Esta semana su hijo está aprendiendo inglés mientras lee acerca de dos hermanos estadounidenses, Wilbur y Orville Wright, quienes inventaron un avión que de verdad podía volar.

En su idioma natal, hablen acerca de lo que conlleva inventar algo: creatividad, imaginación y a veces valentía, como en el caso de los hermanos Wright.

En el Libro de la familia, pida a su hijo que dibuje y escriba acerca de algo que le gustaría inventar. Motive a su hijo a que use su imaginación; el invento no tiene que ser factible.

Esperamos que disfruten de pensar en posibles inventos.

Dear Family Member,

This week your child learned English in another story about the night sky. This is a fantasy about a man who discovers how to make nighttime brighter. He makes stars by poking holes in the night sky!

You and your child might like to observe the night sky again. Perhaps a library book about the stars can help you find more star pictures.

Ask your child why someone might want to make nighttime brighter. He or she might say that it would make it possible to play all night. Encourage your child to write his or her ideas in the Family Book.

We hope you will enjoy more explorations of the night sky.

 Dear Family Member,

This week your child read an old folktale, "The Three Billy Goats Gruff." Three billy goats want to cross a bridge, but they have to get past the troll that lives under it and that wants to eat them.

This story comes from Norway, and perhaps you know it in your home language as well. Talking with your child about such stories can show how the same tale can be told in different ways.

Ask your child to draw the billy goats and the troll in the Family Book and then to write a sentence or two about them.

We hope you will enjoy sharing this and other folktales with your child.

Estimado miembro de la familia:

Esta semana su hijo está aprendiendo inglés con otro cuento acerca del cielo nocturno. Ésta es una fantasía sobre un hombre que descubre cómo iluminar la noche: "hace estrellas" agujereando el cielo nocturno.

Puede que quieran observar la noche de nuevo. Quizás quieran tomar prestado de la biblioteca un libro acerca de las estrellas para encontrar más constelaciones.

Pregunte a su hijo por qué alguien querría iluminar la noche. Respuesta posible: "Se podría jugar toda la noche". Motive a su hijo a anotar sus ideas en el Libro de la familia.

Esperamos que disfruten de más exploraciones de la noche.

Estimado miembro de la familia:

Esta semana su hijo está leyendo un cuento popular en inglés: *The Three Billy Goats Gruff* ("Los tres cabritos Gruff"). Los tres cabritos quieren cruzar un puente sin que los atrape el gnomo que vive debajo, pues se los quiere comer.

Este cuento proviene de Noruega y quizás también lo haya escuchado en su idioma natal. Hablar con su hijo acerca de cuentos como éste puede demostrar cómo se puede contar un mismo cuento de diferentes maneras.

Pida a su hijo que dibuje a los cabritos y al gnomo en el Libro de la familia y que luego escriba una o dos oraciones sobre ellos.

Esperamos que disfruten de compartir éste y otros cuentos populares con su hijo.

Little Duck was flying! He was very
happy.

Invite your child to read aloud "Fly, Little Duck!" Ask:

1. Why was Little Duck sad?

2. How was Big Duck a good friend?

3. What would you like to learn how to do?

8

School–Home Connection

Fold Here

Fly, Little Duck!

by Erica Stanton

1

Fold Here

Little Duck liked to swim. The cold water felt so good on hot days.

Big Duck jumped up and flapped his wings. "Follow me," he said.

Little Duck asked Big Duck to teach him how to fly.

Little Duck wanted to fly, too. He saw his friends in the big blue sky.

Little Duck tried to fly. He jumped up, but he fell on his red beak.

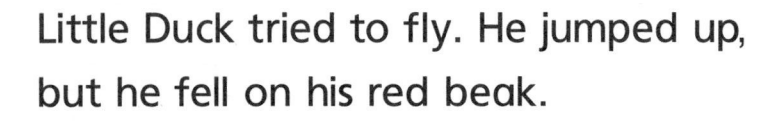

He was sad because he could not fly.

4

5

The Birthday Picnic

by Nancy Ray

My aunt puts candles on the cake. Jill's family and friends all sing "Happy Birthday."

Invite your child to read aloud "The Birthday Picnic." Ask:

1. Who comes to the birthday party?

2. How is the birthday picnic like other birthday parties?

3. What kind of a birthday party would you like to have?

Fold Here

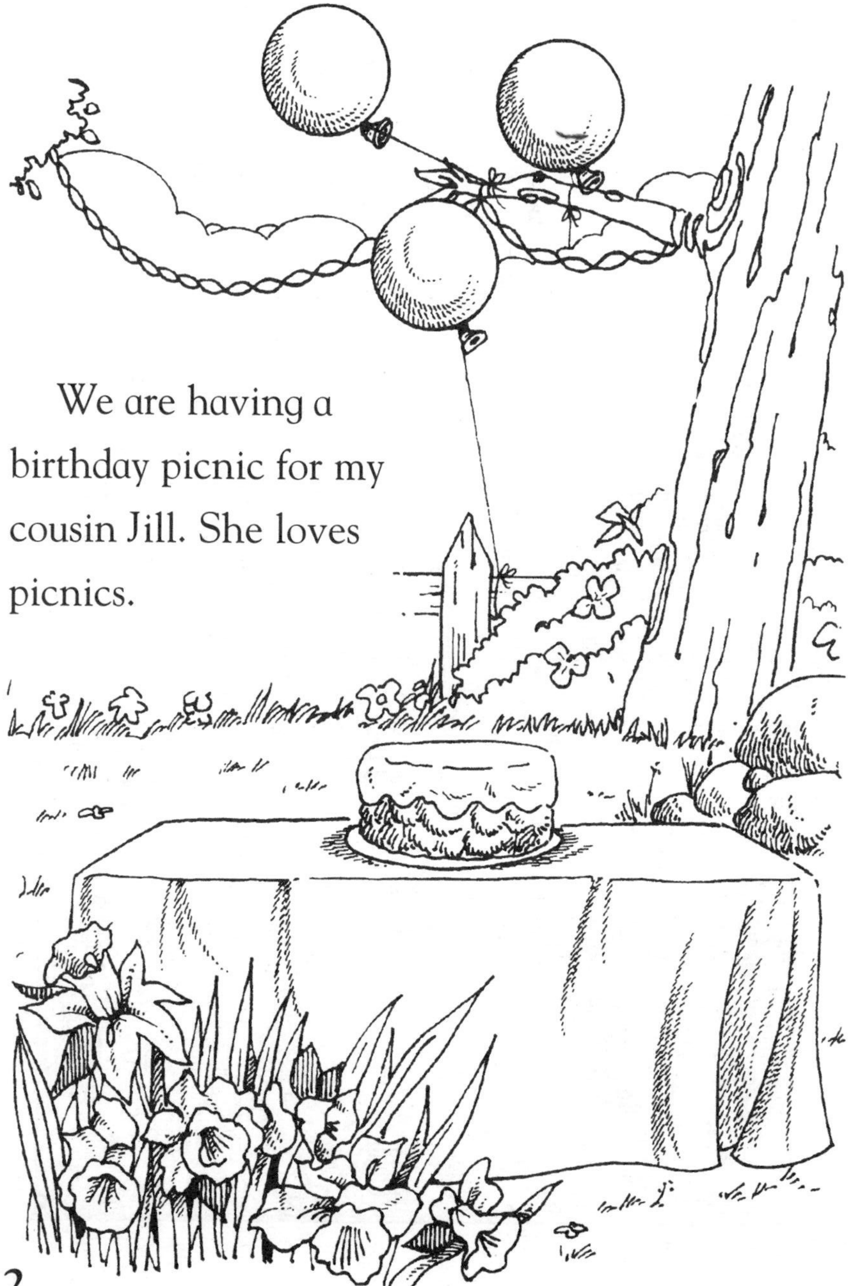

We are having a birthday picnic for my cousin Jill. She loves picnics.

Fold Here

Here is Jill. She is 8 years old today.

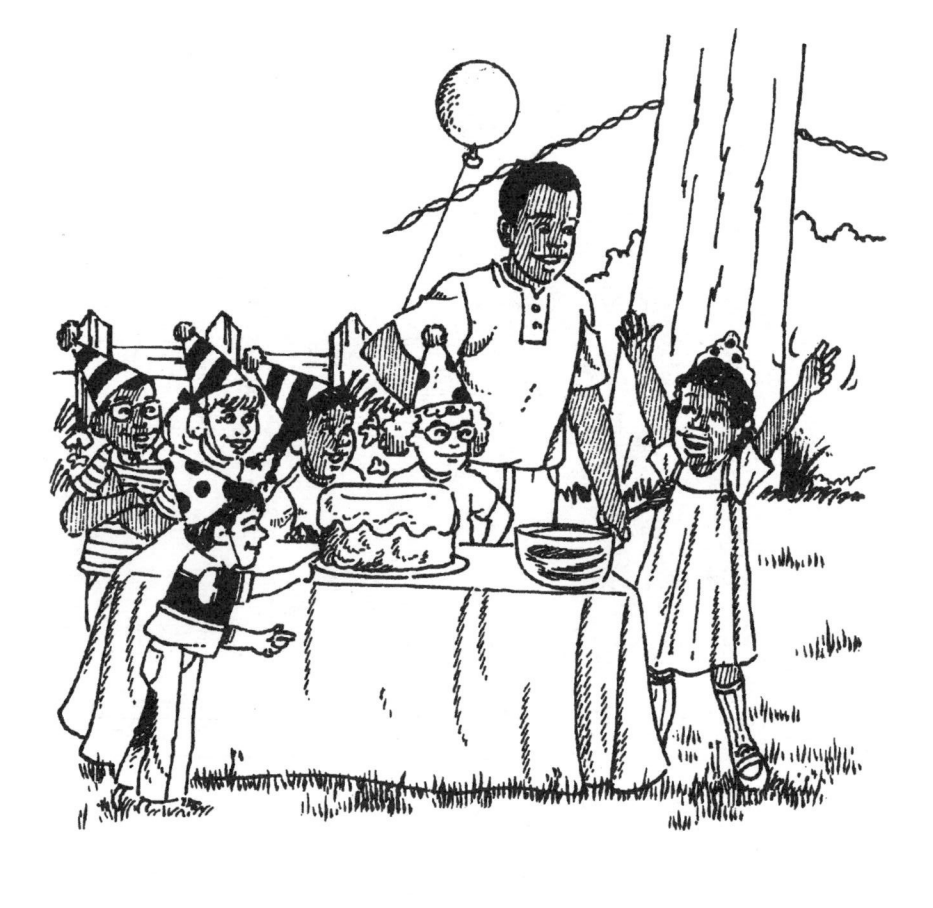

Then we stand near the cake.

My uncle makes lemonade for us to share.

Everyone wears a hat.

We all play games.

Fold Here

Pony went to Mouse's home at the end of the day. Mouse wanted his mom to meet his new friend.

Invite your child to read aloud "New School, New Friends." Ask:

1. How did Mouse and Pony become friends?

2. How is Mouse's school like your school?

3. What do you like to do with your friends at school?

8

Fold Here

New School, New Friends

by Jared Jansen

1

Mouse was walking to his new school.

It was a long walk.

Mouse and his friends made music.

They used paint to make pictures.

Fold Here

Mouse met many other friends.
School was as much fun as a party.

He met Pony on his way. "You may
ride on my back," said Pony.

Fold Here

Mouse held onto Pony. They passed children riding bikes. They got to school very fast.

"Thanks," said Mouse. "That was much faster than walking."

It's a peach pie! My favorite!

Invite your child to read aloud "The Peach Farm."
Ask:

1. What does the girl do at the farm?

2. Why does the girl like going to the peach farm?

3. What is your favorite food?

8

Fold Here

The Peach Farm

by Molly Strong

1

We are going to the peach farm. We put our baskets in the car. We buckle our seat belts to be safe.

When we get back home, Mom tells us to go outside and swim. She is making something special with the peaches.

The weather is hot. We sit in the shade and eat a peach. Peaches are my favorite food!

We get to the farm and grab our baskets. I like to breathe the clean air.

Fold Here

A lot of peaches grow on the trees at the farm. The branches are full.

Dad shows us the best peaches to pick. We fill our baskets.

4

5

Finally, I went to my room. Max was there! I was so happy that I gave him a treat.

Invite your child to read aloud "Where Is Max?" Ask:

1. Where did Max go?

2. Why was the girl sad?

3. How would you feel if you were the girl?

8

Where Is Max?

by Liane B. Onish

Fold Here

I

My dog Max is big and strong. I
know that he is healthy, because he
likes to play.

2

Then, I checked the fence to see if it
was broken. I was very sad.

Fold Here

Next, I looked in the barn. I saw the chickens, but I did not see Max.

One morning, Max jumped out the window. I was not worried, because there is a fence around our yard.

I helped Mom and Dad clean the yard until the afternoon. Then I looked for Max. It was time to feed him.

First, I looked in his doghouse. I could not find him.

4

5

Our New House

by Beverly Tyler

At last, our house was finished. I am proud to live in such a beautiful home!

Invite your child to read aloud "Our New House." Ask:

1. What jobs do workers do to build a house?

2. Why do people need to work together to build a house?

3. What jobs have you seen workers do?

Fold Here

8

1

Last year, workers came to build our new house. First they made the land flat. Big trucks came to carry away the dirt.

Fold Here

The workers put on the roof. Then they painted the house.

Every week my family looked at the plans for the building. We wanted it to be finished!

A team of workers poured the concrete.

Other teams worked together to build the walls of the house.

A crane lifted things that were too heavy for the workers to carry.

Fold Here

A vet comes to the store. He takes time to examine each animal. Sometimes he gives the animals medicine. He makes sure that they stay healthy.

Invite your child to read aloud "The Pet Store." Ask:

1. Why is owning a pet store a lot of work?

2. Why do you think a person would want to own a pet store?

3. Which pet would you want to have? Why?

8

Fold Here

The Pet Store

by Torré Montero

1

Owning a pet store is fun. It is also a lot of work. The animals need someone to care for them.

This mouse eats seeds, as birds do. Mice also need pieces of carrots and lettuce to eat.

These playful puppies need to eat three times a day. Someone also has to take them out of their cage so they can run. Running keeps them healthy.

This frog needs water to drink and rocks to sit on. It needs worms and flies to eat.

Fold Here

This goldfish needs clean water and fish food. It is important to give a fish only a little food at a time. Too much food can make it sick.

Fold Here

These birds need a big cage. Birds need a place to sit, seeds to eat, and clean water to drink.

4

5

When Bunny got home, she said, "I made a big mistake. I will remember to listen to my mother from now on!"

Invite your child to read aloud "Bunny's Big Mistake." Ask:

1. What was Bunny's big mistake?

2. Why do you think Bunny wanted to go over the hill?

3. Did you ever make a big mistake? What happened?

8

School–Home Connection

Fold Here

Bunny's Big Mistake

MAIL

by Susannah Brin

1

Bunny was not happy. She had always wanted to go over the hill.

"You can't go until you are older," said Bunny's mother. "You will only find trouble."

Then a big dog barked at her. The bee, the duck, and the dog all chased Bunny.

The duck chased Bunny, too. She ran into a house. Bunny began to tremble. She was afraid.

Bunny didn't listen to her mother. One morning, Bunny crawled out from under her blanket. She opened the window and climbed down a long ladder.

Bunny walked to the top of the hill. She said, "I'm here, and I did not find any trouble."

Just then a bee flew out of a tree.

The bee chased Bunny. She ran and fell into a pond. A duck lived there.

Fold Here

Fold Here

I dream that I am riding on the train instead of the bus. I'm glad we went on the field trip.

Invite your child to read aloud "The Field Trip." Ask:

1. What do the children learn about trains?

2. Why do you think more people now travel in cars than trains?

3. Where would you like to go on a field trip? Why?

The Field Trip

by Marcel Black

Miss Martinez tells the class that we are going on a field trip. I wonder where we will go.

At the end of the day, we take the bus back to school. Miss Martinez teaches us an old song about working on a railroad.

Fold Here

Miss Martinez tells us that some trains carry people. Other trains carry products made in factories.

We take a school bus. We drive on highways for a long time. Then we drive beside a lake.

"Look at the dam," says Miss Martinez.
"It holds the water in the lake."
I wonder if we are going on a boat.

Fold Here

No! We stop at the train station. Everyone
is excited.

4

5

When the rain stopped, Frog's friends came to his house. "We're sorry we didn't listen to you," they said.

"Storms can be very dangerous," Frog said. "I'm glad that you are all safe."

Invite your child to read aloud "Weather Report." Ask:

1. How does Frog learn about the storm?

2. Why does Frog warn his friends about the storm?

3. How would you prepare for a storm?

School–Home Connection

Fold Here

WEATHER REPORT

by Leigh Holliday

Frog was watching some weather reports on TV. The reporters showed weather maps on their computers. "We'll get a lot of rain today," Frog said.

The wind began to blow, and the leaves began to spin in the air. Soon rain began to fall. Lightning flashed in the sky, and the thunder was very loud.

Frog and his family were safe inside their house, but Frog's friends got wet.

Then Frog went home to help his family prepare for the storm. Mr. Frog closed the windows. Mrs. Frog carried her small pots inside.

"Here comes the storm," said Frog.

Frog went to tell Bird. "A storm is coming," he said.

Bird didn't believe him. "Frog, you can't predict the weather," she said.

Frog went to tell Bear. "A storm is coming," he said.

Bear didn't believe him. He said, "Frog, it is a beautiful day. I'm going to sit under the tree."

Frog went to tell his other friends. They didn't believe him either.

4

5

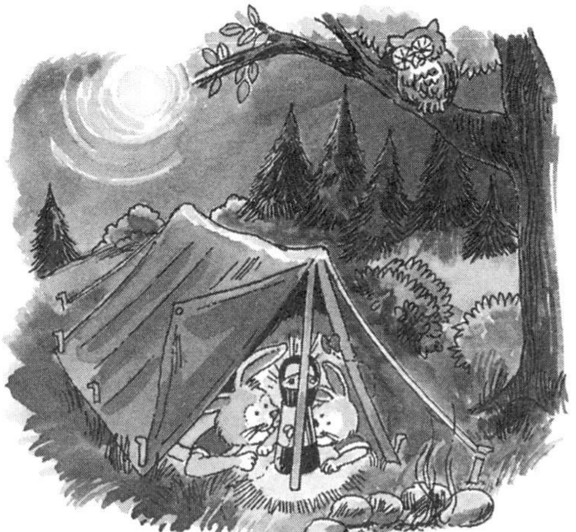

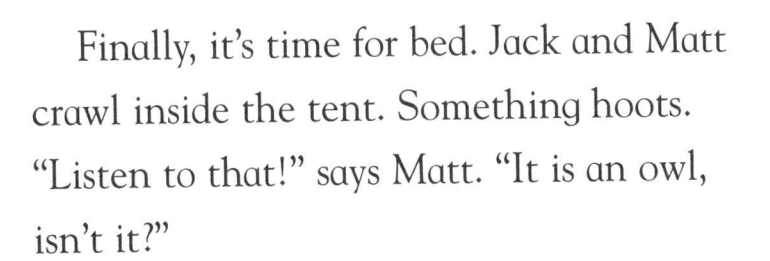

Finally, it's time for bed. Jack and Matt crawl inside the tent. Something hoots. "Listen to that!" says Matt. "It is an owl, isn't it?"

Invite your child to read aloud "Camping Trip." Ask:

1. What things do Jack and Matt do on their camping trip?
2. What are some of the sounds that Jack and Matt hear?
3. Where would you like to go on a camping trip? Why?

Fold Here

School-Home Connection

Camping Trip

by Wendy Young

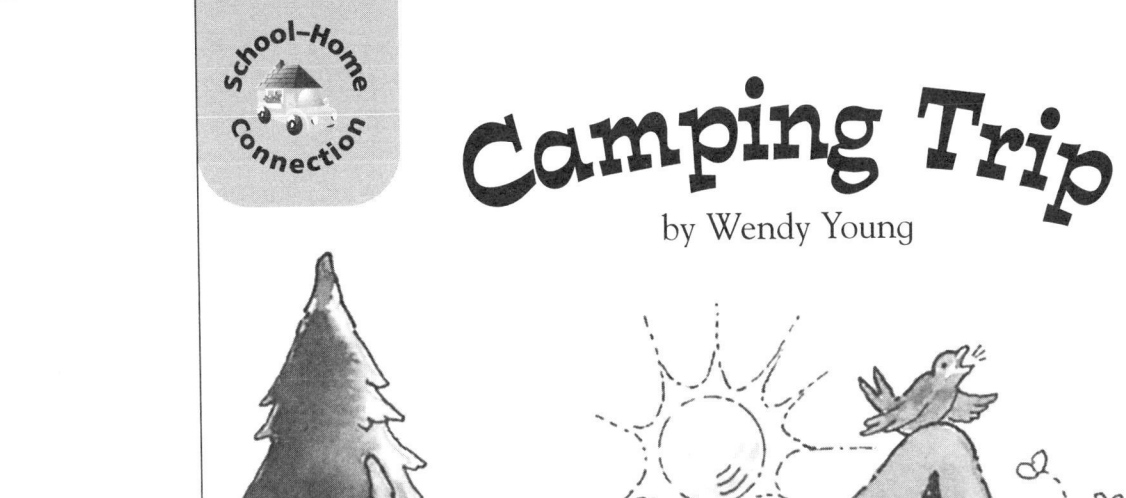

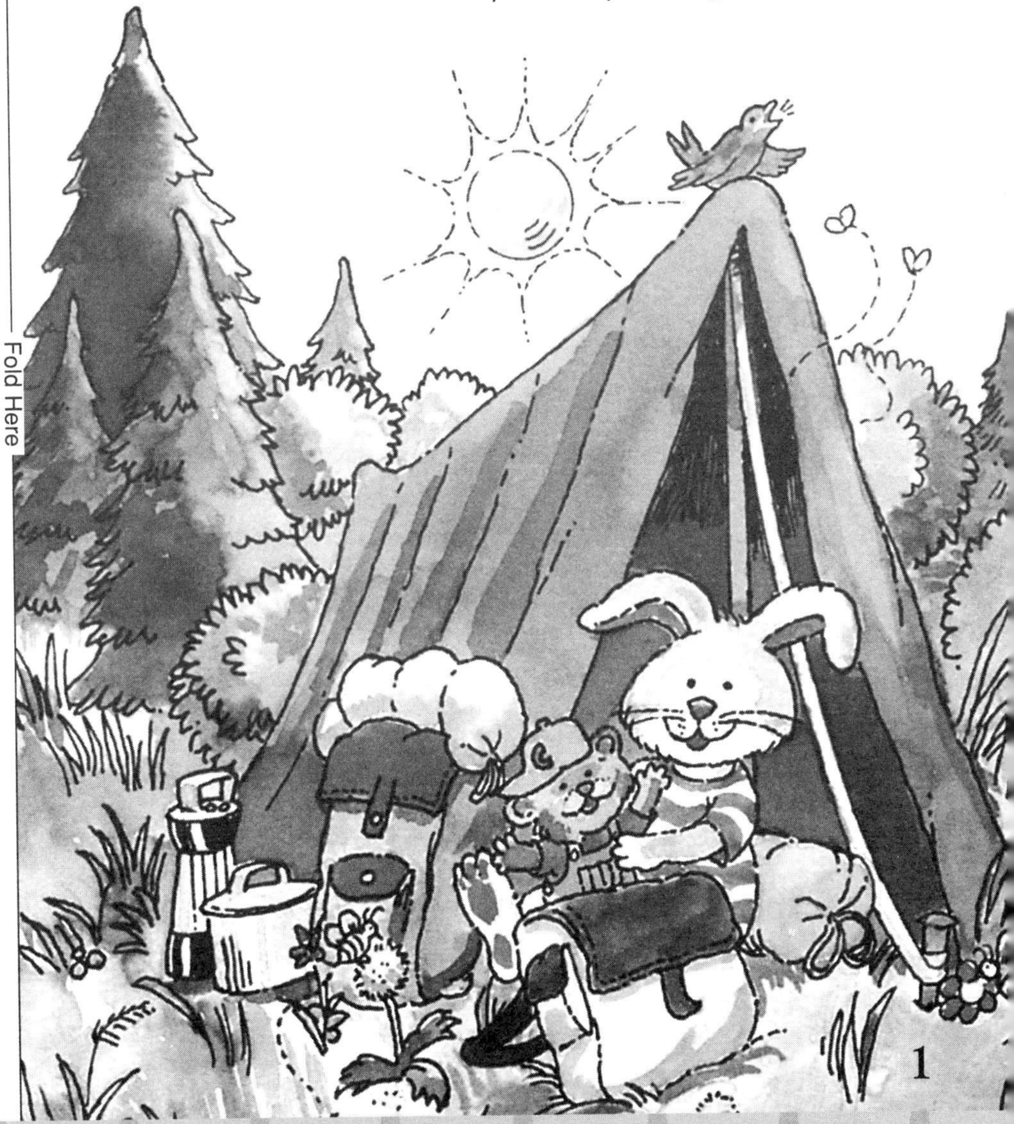

During every summer, Jack and Matt go on a trip. Sometimes they go sailing on the sea. This summer they are going camping.

2

They toast marshmallows and sing a song. They hear the sounds of frogs and bugs nearby. "Listen to that," says Matt.

7

After dinner, Jack and Matt sit by the campfire. The moon and stars shine in the sky.

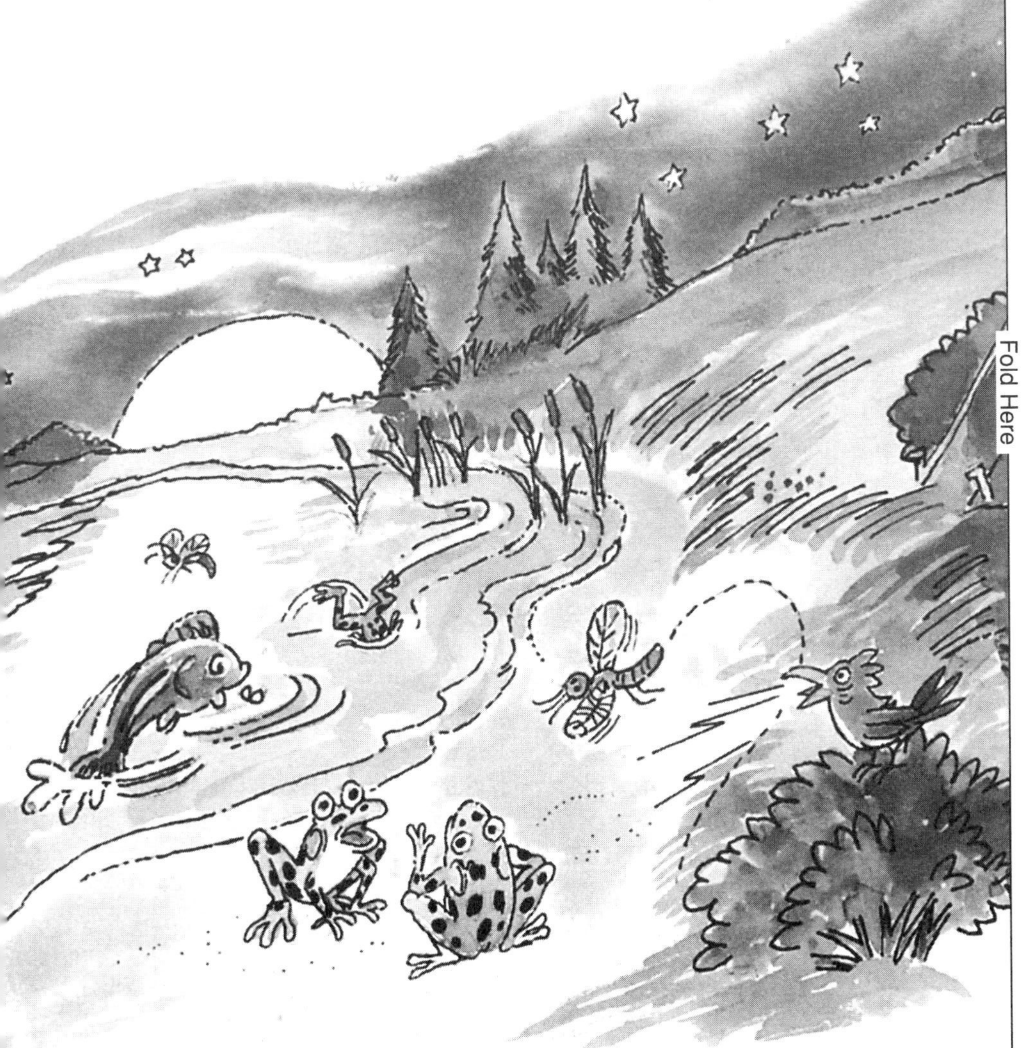

Fold Here

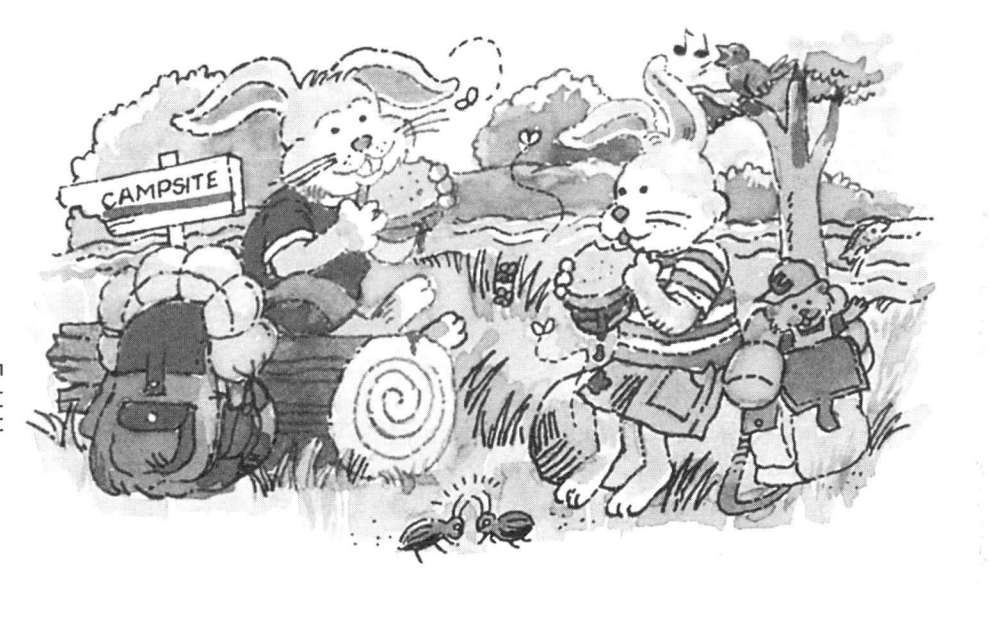

At noon, they stop in a field to eat their lunch. The birds are singing. The flies are buzzing. "Listen to that," says Matt.

At sunset, Matt makes a fire. Jack sets up the tent. It will keep them dry if there is a rain shower. Sleeping in tents is like sleeping under big umbrellas.

They cook dinner on the campfire. The heat from the fire makes the water hiss. "Listen to that," says Matt.

School–Home Connection

Fold Here

Marcy's Lemon Tree

by Holly Miller

"All this work has made me hungry,"
Marcy said to her dog. "One day soon
we will have a big piece of lemon pie!"

Invite your child to read aloud "Marcy's Lemon Tree."
Ask:

1. What is Marcy's problem?

2. How does Marcy solve her problem?

3. What kind of tree would you like to grow? Why?

Marcy was happy. "I will let the soil get dry from now on."

"If you do, the tree will grow juicy lemons," said Marcy's uncle.

Marcy went out in her yard to check on her favorite lemon tree. She had taken it out of a flowerpot and planted it in the ground. It wasn't healthy.

2

7

Marcy's uncle looked at the tree again. He felt the ground.

"Marcy, lemon trees do not like wet soil," he said. "Do not give it so much water."

6

Marcy called her uncle. "Can you tell me what is wrong?" she asked.

"I'll come over and look at it," he said.

Fold Here

3

Marcy and her uncle looked at the tree.

"This is a surprise," he said. "My lemon trees grow well."

"Can you help?" Marcy asked.
"I think I can," her uncle said.

4

5

My mother likes to read my books. She helps me make them better. She's my editor! Mom says, "My Alicia writes and illustrates books. I think I will see one of her books in a bookstore one day."

Invite your child to read aloud "I Love to Draw." Ask:

1. What kinds of things does Alicia like to draw?

2. Why would you need to do research about something you want to draw?

3. Would you like to illustrate books when you grow up? Why or why not?

8

School–Home Connection

Fold Here

I Love to Draw

by T. Ernesto Bethancourt

1

Fold Here

My name is Alicia. I love to draw. When I grow up, I want to illustrate books.

Sometimes I make a little book about something that happened long ago. First I make a diagram of the different pages. I use the information I found in the library books to draw pictures. Then I write about them.

I also like to draw pictures of things that happened long ago. Sometimes I have to find out more about these things first. I go to the library to do research. I find books that tell me what I need to know.

6

Sometimes I draw pictures of things I have done. I like to ride on sleds, so I draw a sled. First I remember what it was like. Then I make a sketch with my pencil.

Fold Here

3

Fold Here

4

Sometimes I draw pictures of places I have never seen. I think about what it would be like to go underwater. I think about sailing on a boat. Then I make a sketch of what I am thinking about.

5

Now Andy plays the guitar all the time. Even the cat likes listening to him play. At night the cat sits on the bed listening until it falls asleep.

Invite your child to read aloud "Andy Plays the Guitar." Ask:

1. Why do you think Andy's dad let him try something different?

2. What else could Andy have learned to play?

3. Have you ever tried to learn how to play something? Tell about it.

8

Andy Plays the Guitar

by Emily Hutchinson

Fold Here

1

Andy was learning to play the violin. His music sounded terrible! Even the cat ran out to the porch when Andy began to play. The cat would run away even if Andy had just poured it a bowl of milk.

Andy and Dad sat in the park. First Dad played a little. Then he handed the guitar to Andy. Andy tried to play. It didn't sound terrible. It sounded quite good!

Fold Here

2

7

Andy and Dad walked home with the guitar.

"I played the guitar when I was a boy," Dad said. "Let's stop at the park. I'll show you how to play it."

"Andy," Dad said one day. "I've been thinking about this for quite a long time. Perhaps the violin isn't for you."

Andy stopped playing and stood there. "Then what should I play?" he asked.

"Let's go to the music store and see what you like," Dad said.

Fold Here

Fold Here

The next day Andy and Dad went to the music store. Andy looked at the drums. He looked at the trumpet. He looked at everything. He thought and thought, but he couldn't decide what he wanted to try.

Finally, the store owner pointed to a guitar.

"Perhaps a guitar would be good for you," he said.

Andy thought about it. "I'll give it a try," he said.

Mom was happy to see her husband and son again. She loved the pottery we brought her. She says that next year she'll come with us, too. I can't wait to go back to the desert!

Invite your child to read aloud "A Trip to the Desert." Ask:

1. What is a desert like?

2. Do you think it would be easy to live in a desert? Why or why not?

3. What place would you like to visit? Why?

8

Fold Here

A Trip to the Desert

by Rachel Glen

1

My father and his friend Jim are scientists. Every summer Dad goes on a trip to study the desert. This year he is taking me with him. We'll be away for two weeks.

2

Dear Mom,

We're getting ready to drive back home now. We're bringing a special present for you! It's some pottery made by a famous Native American woman who lives near here. The pottery is decorated with beautiful designs. See you soon,

Ken

Fold Here

Dear Mom,

It's very hot in the desert. Here is Dad cooling off in the lake near Jim's house. It's the only lake I've seen since I've been here. There isn't much water in the desert.

See you soon,

Ken

6

Dear Mom,

This is Jim's house, where we are staying. Jim studies the ancient people who used to live in the desert.

See you soon,

Ken

Fold Here

3

Dear Mom,

Jim raises a few sheep. They eat the little bit of grass that grows in the desert. In the spring, Jim gets wool from the sheep.

See you soon,

Ken

Fold Here

Dear Mom,

This is a picture of Jim's horse. Its name is Rusty. Sometimes Jim lets me ride Rusty. I pretend I'm a famous cowboy from a long time ago.

See you soon,

Ken

Joe goes to work. He can unload records from the shelves and stack them on the record player. In between playing the records, he does what he likes best . . . talk, talk, talk!

Invite your child to read aloud "Joe's Problem." Ask:

1. What things is Joe good at?

2. Why do you think Joe's friends want to cure him?

3. Do you think Joe's friends found a good way to solve his problem? Explain.

School-Home Connection

Fold Here

Joe's Problem

by Jean Groce

Joe is a special kind of bird. He draws like an artist and likes to create poems. He even bakes cakes. The wonderful smell of those cakes drifts out of his kitchen window. What Joe likes best is talking.

2

"We are looking for someone to do a radio show for us," Ms. Crane says. "We need someone who can play music and do a lot of talking."

"It sounds like the perfect job for me," says Joe.

7

Joe's friends tell him about a job at the radio station. Joe goes there to see if they will hire him.

Fold Here

Do you want to know how to get to Jungle Street?

The problem with Joe is that he can't stop talking. He wants to talk to everyone as he walks across town. He guides birds to places, even if they don't ask for help. He tells others what to do.

Look both ways before you fly across the street.

© Harcourt

He says hello and talks to birds he doesn't know. He stops and buys birdseed in the market just because he wants to talk to someone.

Joe's friends like him very much, but they wish he wouldn't talk so much. They think and think about a way to cure him. Finally, they have an idea.

4

5

When it was time to leave, I was sorry that our trip was over. I will always remember it. I hope that Mom and I can come back soon.

Invite your child to read aloud "Our Holiday Trip." Ask:

1. What do the girl and her mother see on their trip?

2. Why do you think the girl's mother wants her to see what the Netherlands is like?

3. Where would you like to go on a trip? Why?

8

Fold Here

Our Holiday Trip

by Susannah Brin

1

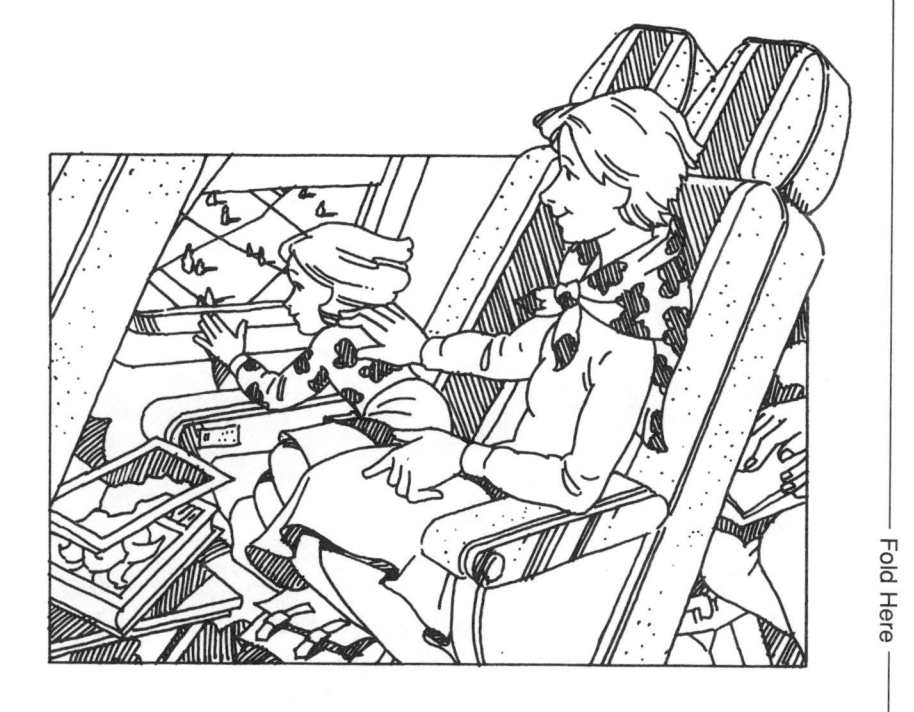

My school was closed for summer vacation. Mom thought it would be a good time to show me the country where she was born. The Netherlands is a long way from the United States, so we had to fly there.

On our last day, we went to the beach again. This time we walked. I watched the boats out on the water.

Fold Here

Fold Here

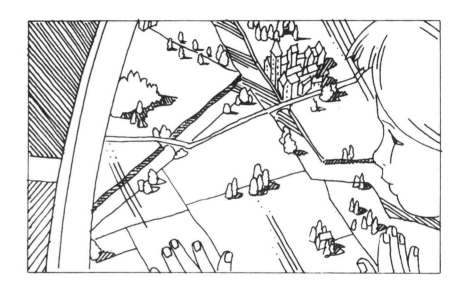

The day after our visit to the beach was an important holiday. Lots of people were celebrating. There were many parades. We watched some dancers.

"Look at their clothes," said Mom. "That's what people here wore a long time ago."

On the flight Mom told me all about the Netherlands. She told me about its history and about the people who live there. She told me about its holidays and why people celebrate each one. She also showed me a picture of the country's flag.

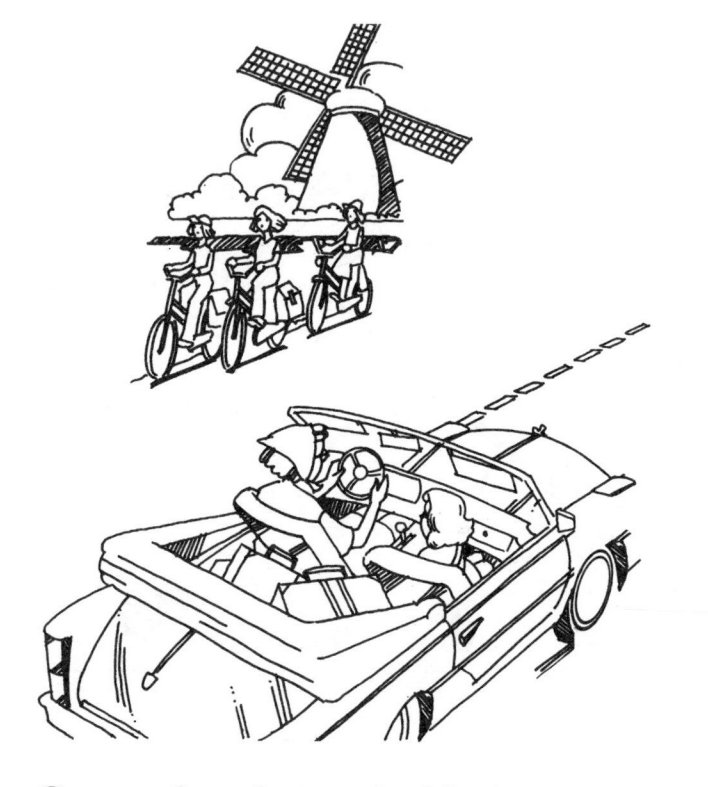

On our first day in the Netherlands, we saw some windmills.

"Windmills were very important here once," Mom said.

"What were they used for?" I asked.

"They were used to pump water," said Mom.

The next day we rented bikes and rode to the beach.

"I remember riding along this beach when I was a child," Mom told me. "It was very windy then, too."

Lou will make many more stops, but we know he will come back to the hospital right on time.

Invite your child to read aloud "Lou's Bus." Ask:

1. Where does Lou's bus stop around the town?

2. Why are buses a good way to travel in a city?

3. What is your favorite way to travel? Why?

8

Lou's Bus

by Patsy Myers

Fold Here

Lou drives a big bus all around our town. Mom and I sometimes ride the bus to the hospital. I need to go there once a month to see my doctors and nurses.

2

We say good-bye and get off the bus. Lou waves and tells us that he will pick us up on his next trip. Then he drives away.

When we get to the hospital, Mom and I get out of our seats. We walk to the front of the bus. Lou stops the bus at the bus stop.

Lou picks up other people along the way. He knows many of the people who live in our neighborhood. As he drives, he waves to the police officers and the mail carriers we pass.

Fold Here

Lou drives past some of the important places in the city. He stops at the post office, the museum, and the courthouse. He stops at the park and the zoo.

People get on and off the bus at the different stops. Some people, like Mr. Leary, take the bus to work. He gets off at the library because he is one of the librarians. Other people take the bus to go shopping or to go to places for fun.

It was late now. Andrew and Jenny had to go home. They waved good-bye to their new friends.

Invite your child to read aloud "A Walk in the Forest." Ask:

1. What do Andrew and Jenny see in the forest?

2. What other things might you see in a forest?

3. Where would you like to take a walk? Why?

Fold Here

School–Home Connection

A Walk
in the
Forest

by Dana Catharine

Andrew and Jenny were walking on a path in the forest. The ground was very damp from the rain. Leaves and sticks crumbled beneath their feet.

Andrew and Jenny were excited about all the things they had seen. They wondered what else they might discover in the forest.

On a tall tree they saw a woodpecker. It was busy pecking on the tree's bark. It was looking for bugs to eat.

Peck, peck, peck!

The bark crumbled as it pecked.

At the end of the path, they discovered a pond. Two beavers were in it. One was carrying sticks in its mouth. The beavers were busy making a dam. It looked like a big mound in the middle of the pond.

6

3

When Andrew and Jenny got closer to the pond, a frog suddenly appeared. It jumped up and sat on a rock. Some plants had sprouted around the rock.

Andrew and Jenny walked along the edge of the pond. Suddenly a feather dropped out of the air. They looked up to see where it had come from.

4

5

Now that you know all about flamingos, I'm going to fly away. I have to meet a flamingo friend of mine. She lives on an island near here. Good-bye!

Invite your child to read aloud "Rosie Flamingo." Ask:

1. What did you learn about flamingos?
2. How do you think a flamingo's long legs help it walk in the water?
3. What kind of bird would you like to learn about? Why?

Fold Here

School-Home Connection

Rosie Flamingo

by Jean Groce

Hello! I'm a special kind of bird called a flamingo. My feathers and bill are pink, just like a rose. That's why I'm called Rosie.

2

Fold Here

About five days after hatching, my baby will waddle from the nest. After a few more weeks, it will be able to find its own food. Soon it will look just like me.

After a month, the egg will hatch. My baby flamingo will have a pink bill, but its feathers will be white and gray.

6

Fold Here

Like all birds, I have two wings. I have a long neck and a large bill. I also have long, thin legs. They make it easy for me to walk in the water to find my food.

3

When I'm hungry, I walk into the water and bend my head upside down. Then I open my mouth like a pouch and let some water in. The tiny plants and animals in the water go down my slippery throat. This morning I waddled into the water and found lots to eat.

Each year I make my nest with mud from the bottom of the lake.

I lay my egg in the mud nest. Then I sit on the egg to keep it warm, even in the most miserable weather. My husband also takes a turn. He likes to snuggle on the egg.

4

5

I wish we could travel into space like astronauts! We can't visit the other planets yet. It would take too much time to get there and back. For now, we can only dream about a vacation in space!

Invite your child to read aloud "Faraway Places."
Ask:

1. Why does the child think about vacations in different places?

2. Which places in the story could you really go to on a vacation?

3. Which place would you like to visit? Why?

8

Fold Here

FARAWAY PLACES

by Beverley Dietz

1

When I'm in bed at night, I think about places my family and I could go on vacation.

I'd like to visit the place where our country fought the first battle for independence. We would learn a lot about our country's history.

We would all enjoy visiting a big city. There would be tall buildings and long bridges there. The streets would be busy with people, cars, and trucks. We could visit museums to see art from around the world.

Fold Here

It would be very different in other countries. The people would eat different foods and speak another language. They would also have different laws.

Fold Here

In winter we could travel to a place where it is very cold. We could play in the snow and skate on the ice. That would be a lot of fun!

We could also travel to a place that is very hot. There would be lots of sand in the desert but hardly any water. We could ride on some of the camels that live there.

I'd love to travel to a place where there are wild animals! We could see monkeys swinging in the tall trees of the rain forest. We could also see many kinds of colorful birds.

Fold Here

Moon had a clever idea. "Come, Small Star," he said. "You can sit on top of my head."

Small Star jumped up and sat on Moon's head. She sits there still, with her shadow falling across Moon's face. That is why the moon is no longer as bright as the sun.

Invite your child to read aloud "Brother Moon, Sister Star." Ask:

1. What was the problem in the story?

2. What are some other ways Moon could have solved the problem?

3. What did you like best about this story?

8

Fold Here

BROTHER MOON, SISTER STAR

Retold by Susannah Brin

1

Native Americans like to tell stories as they sit awake at night. Some of the stories are about the evening sky and the distant stars. This story is about the moon and the small, bright star near the moon.

2

7

At last it was winter. Moon and Small Star looked around their house. They were amazed at how much they had gathered.

"Our house is full of food and presents. I worry that there may not be room for everyone," said Small Star.

Small Star was right. When the sky people came, there was nowhere for Small Star to sit.

Fold Here

Once there was a kind chief who ruled the sky. He was as bright as any star, even the star that is our sun. His name was Moon. He lived in the sky with his gentle sister, Small Star.

© Harcourt

One summer evening, Moon said to Small Star, "This winter I want to have a party for all of the sky people."

"Then we will need to gather lots of food and presents to give to our friends," said Small Star.

All through fall, Moon and Small Star gathered firewood and collected shells for presents. They picked berries, being careful not to get tangled in the bushes. One day Small Star did get tangled. She tumbled down, but she was not hurt.

Fold Here

4

5

Dear Anna,
I'm home.
Let's play!
Your friend,
Pedro.

Invite your child to read aloud "Dear Anna." Ask:

1. What things does Pedro do at the ranch?

2. Do you think the ranch is close to where Pedro lives? Explain your answer.

3. What would you like to do when you grow up?

Fold Here

Dear Anna

by Ben Farrell

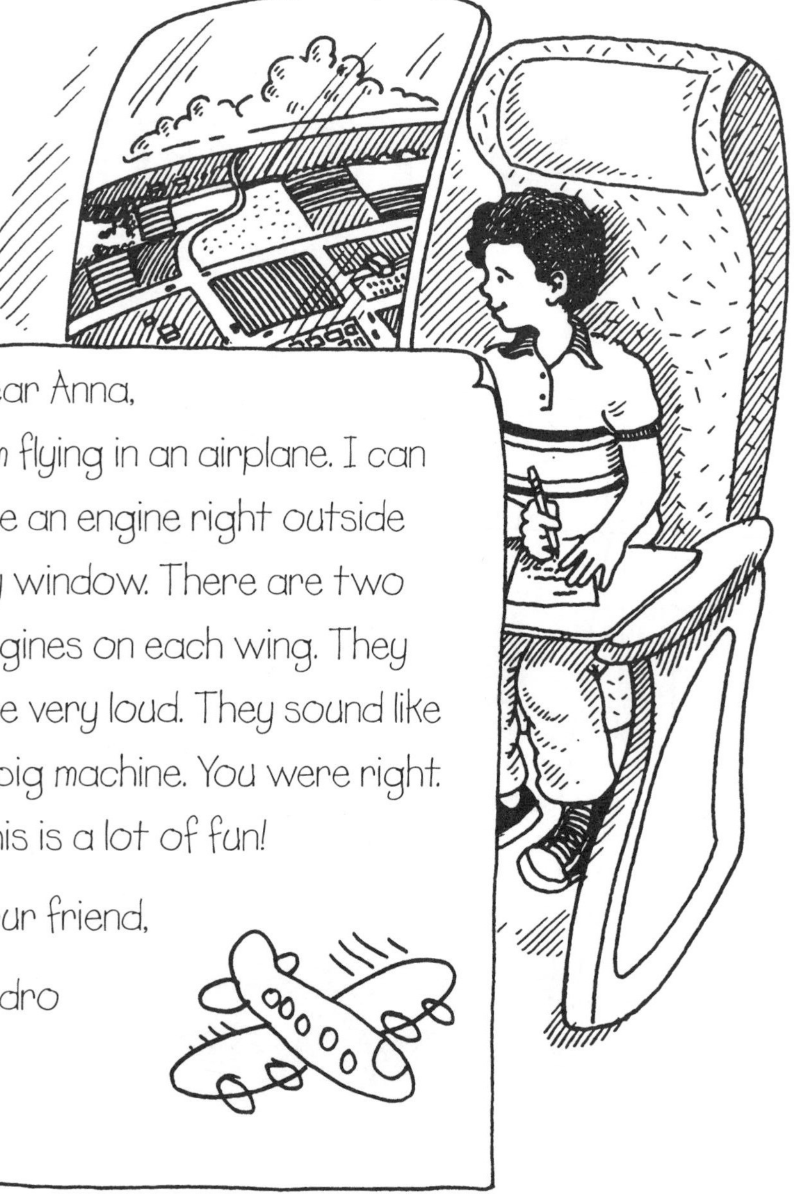

Dear Anna,

I'm flying in an airplane. I can see an engine right outside my window. There are two engines on each wing. They are very loud. They sound like a big machine. You were right. This is a lot of fun!

Your friend,

Pedro

Fold Here

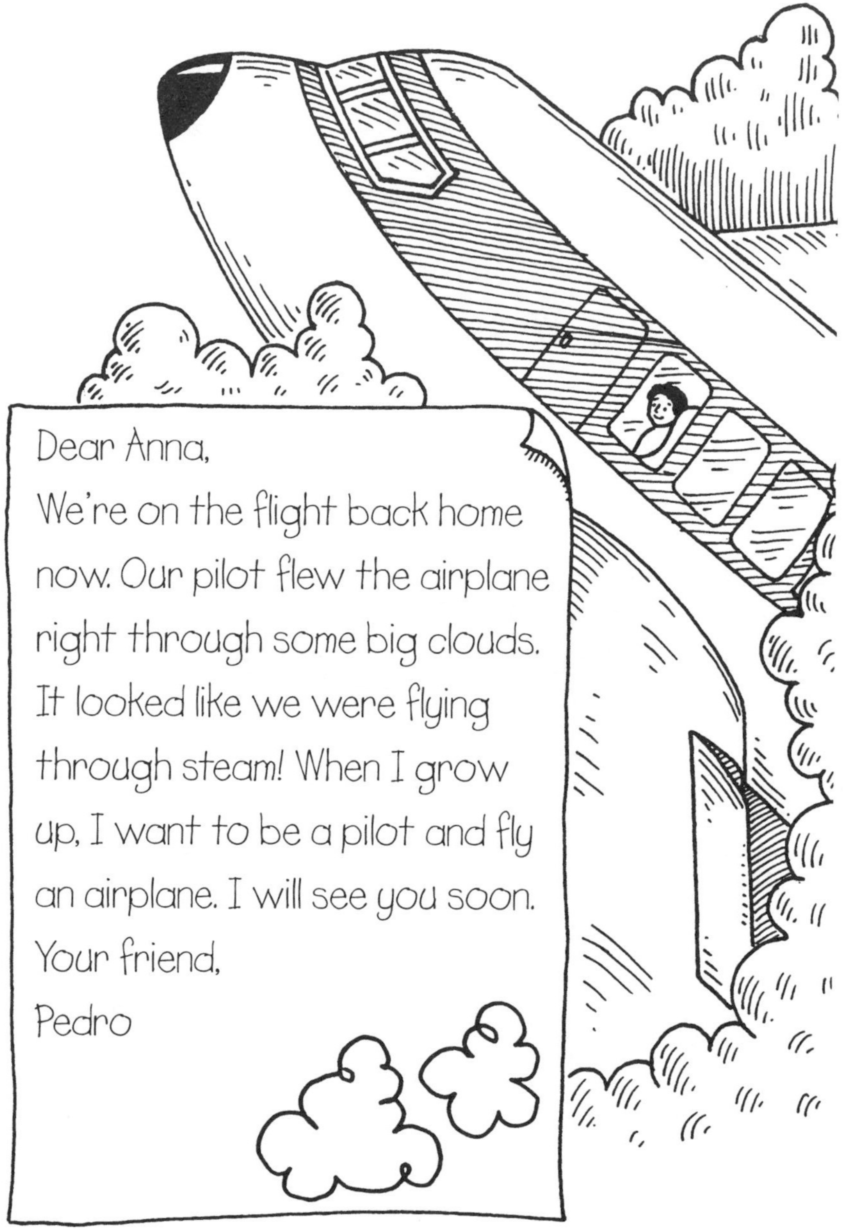

Dear Anna,

We're on the flight back home now. Our pilot flew the airplane right through some big clouds. It looked like we were flying through steam! When I grow up, I want to be a pilot and fly an airplane. I will see you soon.

Your friend,

Pedro

Dear Anna,

Today Mom, Dad, and I drove to a lake not far from my uncle's ranch. We sailed on a boat. The wind was blowing very hard. It made the boat go very fast. I had to hold on tight!

Your friend,

Pedro

Fold Here

Dear Anna,

It's been a long flight, but I can see the airport below us. There are lots of airplanes and a helicopter down there. They look so little from up here. I can't wait to get to my uncle's ranch!

Your friend,

Pedro

Dear Anna,

This afternoon I went for a ride on one of my uncle's horses. We rode all around the ranch. It took a long time to get from one end to the other. We stopped to eat under a tree. It's hot out here.

Your friend,

Pedro

Fold Here

Dear Anna,

Today my uncle and I built a fence for the sheep. It will keep them from running away into the hills. The sheep like to eat the grass on the ranch. I fed them some. The baby lamb ate right out of my hand!

Your friend,

Pedro

Before we went to bed, we had a conversation about Grandpa's story. We knew it wasn't real, but we looked out the window to make sure the moon was still there. We were happy to see it shining in the sky!

Invite your child to read aloud "Grandma's Chair." Ask:

1. What do the children do in Grandma's chair?

2. Why do you think the children look to see if the moon is still there?

3. What kinds of stories does your family tell?

8

School–Home Connection

Grandma's Chair

by Bess Sanders

Fold Here

1

Lucy and I went to our grandparents' house to sleep. When we got there, we jumped into Grandma's big chair. We love her chair. It is so big that the two of us can sit in it together.

2

Before bedtime, we sat on the couch with Grandpa and the cats. One cat sat on the couch's peak. The other cat snuggled with me. Grandpa told us a story. It was about a horrible storm that made the moon disappear. We love Grandpa's stories, even if they are a little scary.

7

Then we all went into the kitchen and helped Grandma cook dinner. After we ate, we helped her clean up and wash the dishes. Then we had cookies for dessert.

We turned off the lamp and put a blanket over us to keep warm. It was very cold outside. We watched the stars as they flickered in the sky.

Fold Here

6

3

Later Grandma sat down with us and read us a story. Lucy sat on one side, and I sat on the other. That way we could both look at the pictures.

Grandpa sat in the chair and pretended to be asleep. We played with his hair and poked him softly. Grandpa pretended to wake up and be surprised.